Super-Duper Science
Ladybug, Ladybug

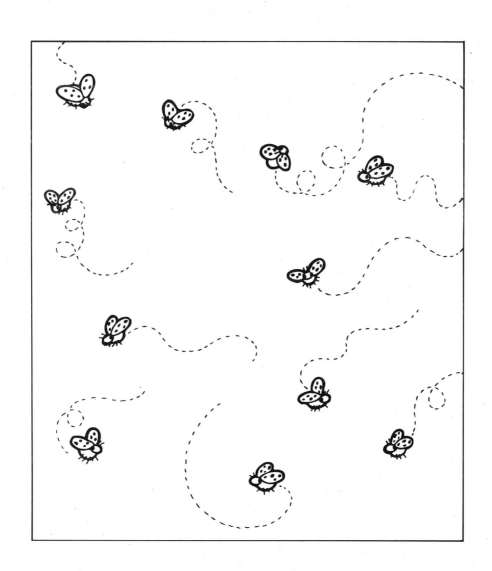

by Annalisa Suid
illustrated by Marilynn G. Barr

For Mark, Jesse, & Brian

Publisher: Roberta Suid
Editor: Carol Whiteley
Design & Production: Susan Pinkerton
Educational Consultant: Sarah Felstiner
Cover Art: Mike Artell

Also by the author: *Save the Animals!* (MM 1964), *Love the Earth!* (MM 1965), *Learn to Recycle!* (MM 1966), *Sing A Song About Animals* (MM 1987), and *Preschool Connections* (MM 1993).

On-line address: MMBooks@AOL.com

P.O. Box 1680, Palo Alto, CA 94302

1-878279-86-6
Printed in the United States of America
987654321

CONTENTS

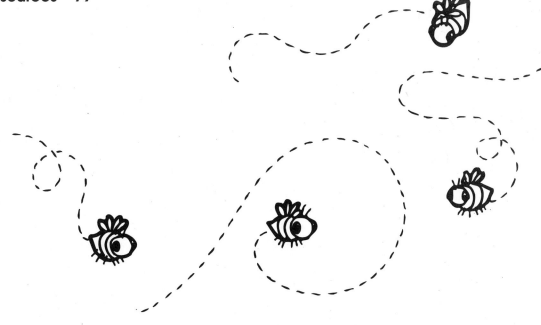

INTRODUCTION

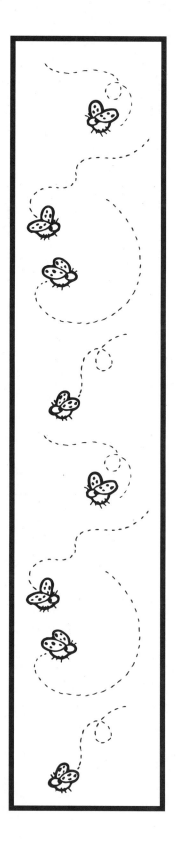

Ladybug, Ladybug is composed of eight chapters, each a complete unit dedicated to a specific insect (except for the spider chapter, which can be used to demonstrate the *differences* between spiders and insects). This book is intended to help children develop a hands-on understanding of science while developing language skills. Children will learn to relate to the insect world in a personal way: learning through games, observations, literature, and art.

Let's Read features a popular children's book, such as *The Grouchy Ladybug* by Eric Carle, and is accompanied by a detailed plot description. **Let's Talk** helps children link the featured book with familiar feelings, thoughts, or ideas in their own lives. For example, in the Bee chapter, the "Let's Talk" discussion focuses on feeling shy. This page also includes a pattern that can be duplicated and used as a bookmark.

Let's Learn is filled with facts about each insect (or spider). For example, common ladybugs have seven spots and are considered friendly by farmers. Choose facts that you think will interest your children. Read a fact a day during the unit.

The **Let's Create** activities in each chapter allow children to use their imaginations. They will make their own insects from craft materials, draw pictures, design flowers, eat snacks, and so on.

Children make a hands-on science connection in the **Let's Find Out** activities. These projects focus on exploration, leading children through moments of discovery as they *find out* what it's like to be on the inside of a cocoon or what fireflies look like as they blink in the night sky.

Let's Play suggests a new game (or games) to interest children in the bug of the moment. A chant or a new song sung to a familiar tune is featured in the **Let's Sing** section. Children can learn the new lyrics and perform them for parents, or each other. Mother Goose rhymes are also included if there's a rhyme about the particular insect (or spider).

Informative **Pattern Pages** complete each chapter. These patterns can be duplicated and used for bulletin board displays, reduced for cubby labels or name tags, or used for desk labeling. (Children can color the patterns using crayons or markers.)

At the end of the book, you'll find a **Storybook Resources** section filled with additional fiction picture- and storybooks, plus a **Nonfiction Resources** section suggesting factual and photograph books of the featured insects. **Additional Resources** includes street and "e-mail" addresses for additional insect information.

ALL ABOUT INSECTS

What Makes a Bug a Bug?

Bugs have segmented body parts (the thorax and the abdomen), front and back wings, six legs, and mouth parts in the form of a beak that can pierce and suck. Some bugs live on dry land, and others live in or near water. Most bugs eat by sucking plant juices. Some suck the blood of other insects and spiders. Others feed on humans and other animals.

Bugs include: ants, aphids, bees, beetles, butterflies, cockroaches, flies, grasshoppers, mosquitoes, moths, wasps.

This is a bug:

Front wings

Antenna

Abdomen

Six legs

Hind wings

This is not a bug ... No wings!

Four pairs of eyes

Eight legs

. . . it's a spider. Spiders are arachnids. Arachnids have four pairs of eyes, eight legs, no wings, spinnerets, and two body sections. A spider's eyes, legs, and jaws are on the front body part. The back part, which is much larger, has a set of little taps called spinnerets.

Let's Read Nonfiction Insect Books:
Bugs: Giant Magnified Images As Seen Through a Microscope by Heather Amery and Jane Songi (A Golden Book, 1994).

CATERPILLARS

Introduction

❀ Let's Read:

The Very Hungry Caterpillar by Eric Carle (Philomel, 1987). A very hungry little caterpillar eats through the week, until it finally is full. Then it spins a cocoon in preparation for becoming a butterfly! Eric Carle's classic colorful tissue paper illustrations are sure to delight your children. They'll enjoy repeating familiar lines while also learning to count and the days of the week.

❀ Let's Talk:

Ask children to remember a time when they were very hungry. Then have them list the foods that they most wanted to eat. Did they crave junk foods or healthy foods? Make a room graph of favorite foods, ranked in order from most to least favorite. Use counting blocks or marks on a paper to show how many children like each kind of food. See if the children share any common favorites with the Very Hungry Caterpillar.

❀ Let's Learn:

Most children have seen butterflies before, but they may not realize that a caterpillar is a "baby" butterfly. All butterflies start life as tiny eggs. Very tiny (and very hungry) caterpillars hatch from the eggs. When a caterpillar has finished growing, it finds a place to rest and build a chrysalis (also called a cocoon). After a certain amount of time (weeks, months, or even years, depending on the type of caterpillar) a butterfly emerges!

Refer to the **Nonfiction Resources** at the end of the book for color pictures of butterfly larva, caterpillars, and full-grown butterflies.

Let's Create: A Caterpillar Feast

The Very Hungry Caterpillar munched on many different kinds of foods, both healthy snacks and junk foods. Discuss with your children the types of foods that make up a balanced diet.

❀ What You Need:
Small paper plates (one per child); plastic spoons and forks; a variety of healthy foods, such as cut-up plums, strawberries, grapes, and bananas

❀ What You Do:
1. Set out a buffet on a long, low table. Place paper plates and plastic utensils at one end, and the plates of food in a row.
2. Encourage children to help themselves to an amount they feel comfortable eating. Or have an aide nearby to assist in serving the children. Just like the caterpillar, they can count how many pieces they take of each kind of fruit.
3. Read *The Very Hungry Caterpillar* during snack time.
4. Then teach the children the caterpillar chant (p. 16). Remind children that in order for them to grow, they need to eat healthy food—just like the Hungry Caterpillar.

Book Links:
• *Young Chef's Nutrition Guide and Cookbook* by Carolyn E. Moore, Mimi Kerr, and Robert Shulman (Barron's, 1990) is a good source of healthy diets for children.
• *Kids Cooking Without a Stove* by Aileen Paul, illustrated by Carol Inouye (Doubleday, 1975), is filled with simple recipes to choose from.

CATERPILLARS

Let's Create: Butterfly Wings

❁ What You Need:
Construction paper in a variety of colors, scissors, crayons, markers, glitter, tape or glue, pipe cleaners

❁ What You Do:
1. Show the children how to cut a butterfly from a folded piece of construction paper. This is similar to cutting a Valentine heart, but the "rounded" shape is done twice. (See illustration.)
2. Provide crayons and markers for children to use to decorate their butterfly wings. Children can also use glitter and glue to make their butterflies sparkle.
3. Show children how to glue or tape two bent pipe cleaners to the back of the butterfly to make antennae.
4. Post completed pictures on a "Beautiful Butterfly" bulletin board.

Option: Cover the bulletin board ahead of time with flower-patterned wrapping paper, or cut out flowers from construction paper for the butterflies to "land" on.

Note: This would be an appropriate time to discuss "B" words, such as bug, bumblebee, and beetle.

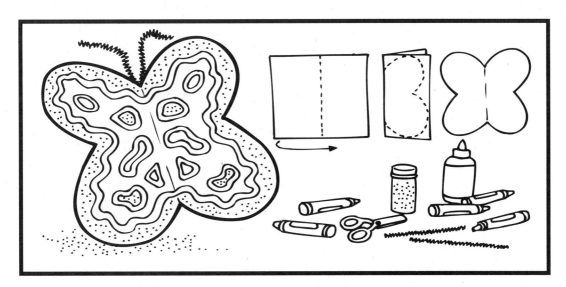

Let's Create: Butterfly Dresses & Caterpillar Suits

Butterflies are beautiful insects that come in a wide range of colors. Caterpillars are also very unique: spotted, striped, and multicolored. Your children can make their own colorful clothing for "paper doll" butterflies and caterpillars to wear.

❀ What You Need:

Paper doll patterns (p. 11), clothes patterns (pp. 12-13), scissors, heavy paper, crayons or markers, straws, glitter, glue, tape (optional)

❀ What You Do:

1. Duplicate the butterfly and caterpillar paper doll patterns onto heavy paper and cut out. Make one for each student.
2. Duplicate the clothing patterns and cut out. (Older children may be able to cut out the patterns themselves.) Provide one of each style for each student.
3. Let the children color in the clothing patterns. They can use markers, crayons, glitter and glue, and so on.
4. While the clothes are drying, children can glue one straw to the back of their butterfly or caterpillar pattern to use for a handle.
5. When the clothing patterns are dry, children can dress their paper dolls in the different outfits, and stage an insect fashion show. Older children can use the tabs to fasten and refasten the outfits. Younger children may simply tape the clothing to the paper dolls for a permanent look.

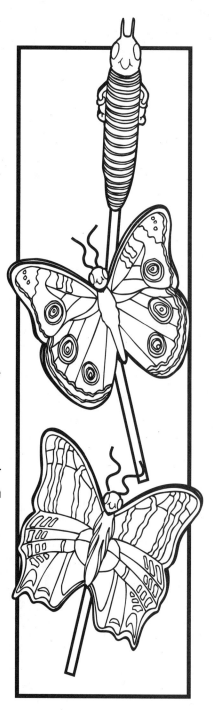

PAPER DOLL PATTERNS

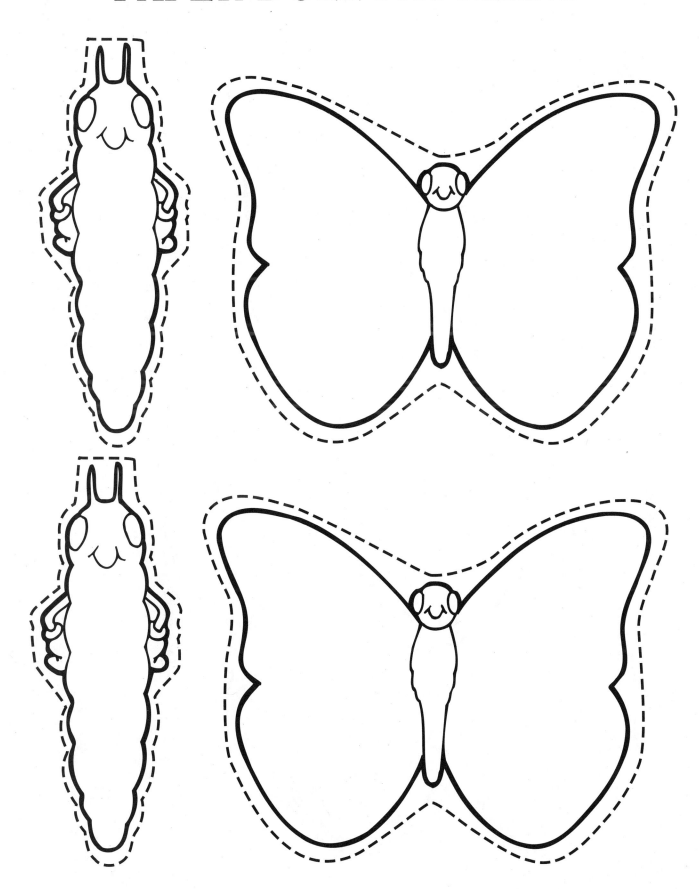

PAPER DOLL CLOTHING

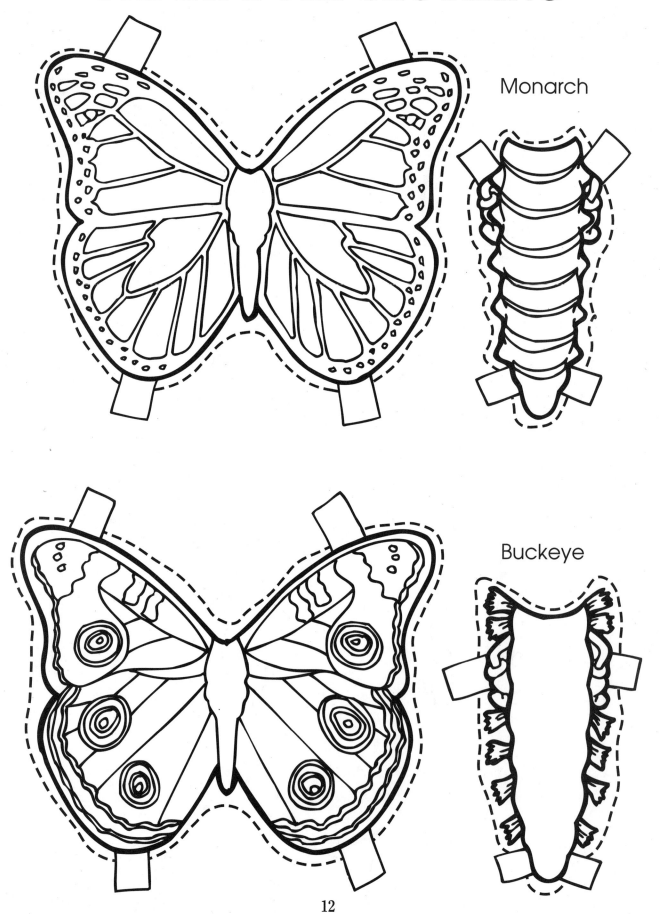

Monarch

Buckeye

~ PAPER DOLL CLOTHING ~

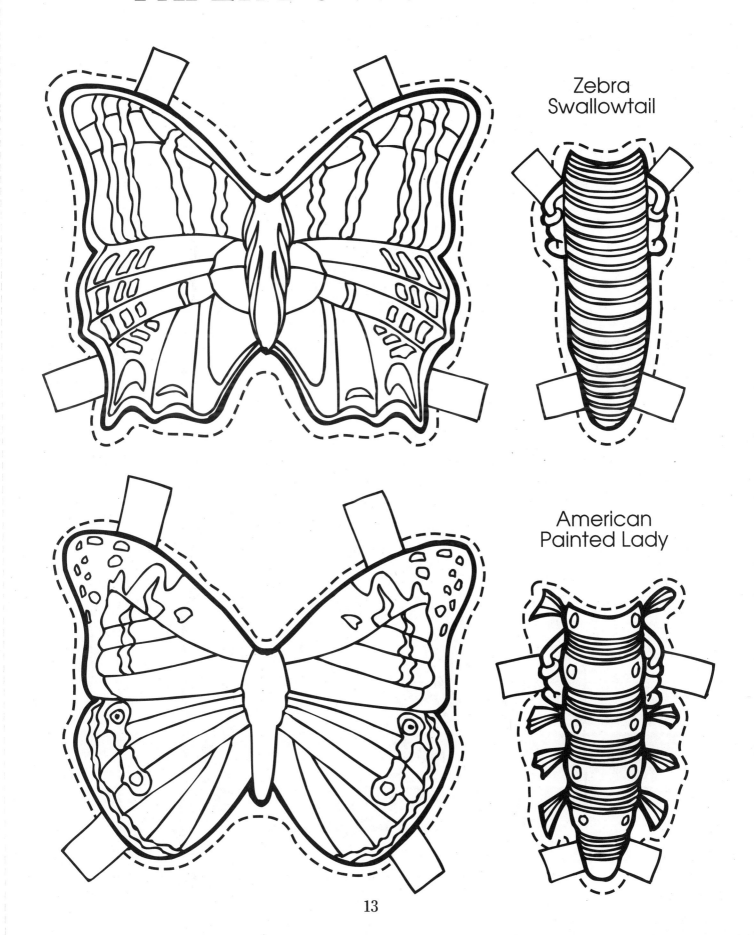

Zebra
Swallowtail

American
Painted Lady

13

CATERPILLARS

Let's Find Out: About the Inside of a Cocoon

❀ **What You Need:**
Toilet paper

❀ **What You Do:**
1. Divide the children into teams of two.
2. Give each team a roll of toilet paper.
3. Have one child in each team pretend to be a caterpillar, while the other child assists and loosely wraps the "caterpillar" in its toilet paper cocoon. (Have the children wrap only to the shoulders. They should not cover the head of the caterpillar!)
4. When the caterpillars are all wrapped, have them close their eyes and imagine that they are about to become butterflies.
5. Have the caterpillars stretch their wings and tear through the toilet paper cocoons.
6. Collect the discarded toilet paper (for use in another project), and then let the partners switch roles.
7. After everyone has had a chance to metamorphose, ask the children the following questions to find out how they felt when they were wrapped up: "Did you like being in such a small place?" "Would you want to live in a cocoon for weeks (or months) the way a caterpillar does?" "How did you feel when you broke free?"
8. Let the newly hatched butterflies spread their wings and fly around the room.

CATERPILLARS

Let's Play: Caterpillar Tag

❀ What You Need:
Nothing

❀ What You Do:
1. Choose one child to be the leader of the caterpillar.
2. The rest of the children are "free agents," and run away from the leader, who tries to tag them.
3. When a child is tagged, he or she joins onto the caterpillar leader by placing one hand on the leader's shoulder. The other hand can be used to try to tag other children.
4. As more children are tagged, they join the chain, always keeping one hand on the shoulder of the child in front.
5. The last child tagged can be the lead caterpillar in the next round.

Let's Play: Butterfly Relay Race

❀ What You Need:
Construction paper, scissors, tape

❀ What You Do:
1. Cut out flower shapes from construction paper.
2. Set or tape the flowers along one wall of the room.
3. Divide children into three- or four-person relay teams.
4. Have the children stand opposite the wall of flowers.
5. Explain that the goal of the game is to "fly" (the children can flap their arms) to a flower, tag it, and "fly" back to the team. Each butterfly in turn takes a turn, until everyone on a team has touched a flower.

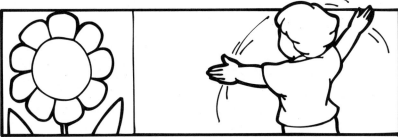

CATERPILLARS

Let's Sing: Caterpillar Chant

A caterpillar looks so small.
It is hardly there at all.
It munches on green leafy treats,
And it gets bigger as it eats.

It eats and eats, 'til pretty soon,
It wraps up tight in a cocoon.
When it wakes up it blinks its eyes
And says, "I'm now a butterfly!"

Let's Sing: Butterfly Chant

A burst of blue,
A shock of green,
A flap of wings is all that's seen.
A flutter in the flower beds,
A burst of blue,
A bit of red,
A whisper as it flutters by,
You're oh so pretty, butterfly.

"I'M A CATERPILLAR"

"I'M A BUTTERFLY"

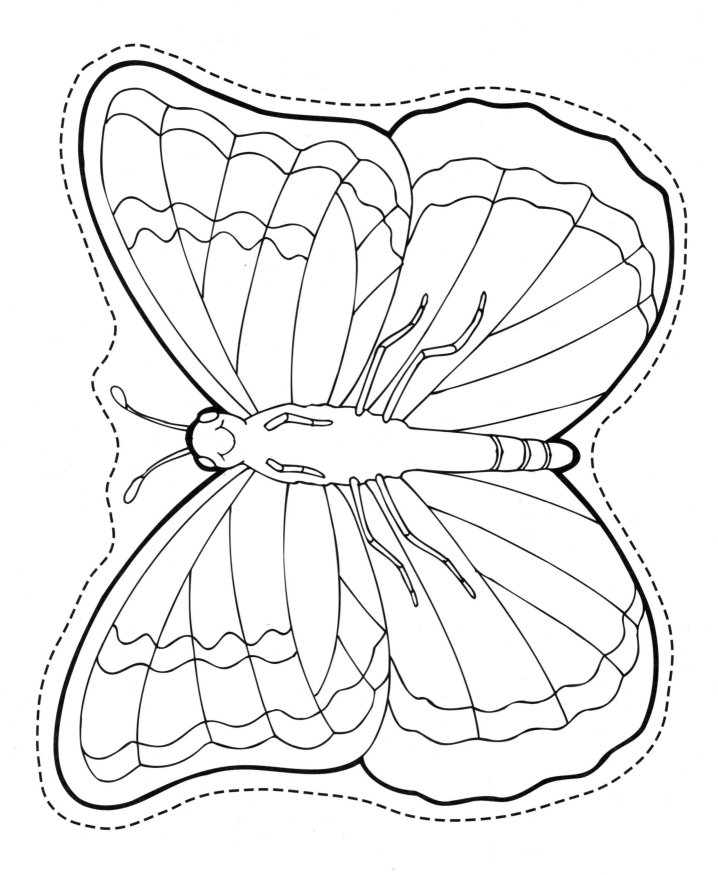

CRICKETS

Introduction

❀ Let's Read:
The Very Quiet Cricket by Eric Carle (Putnam, 1990).
The cricket in this story is not able to make a sound. When he is greeted by many insects, he tries to respond to each one but can't. Finally, at the end of the book, he meets a lady cricket, and he sings for her the most beautiful song she has ever heard! (This book has a mechanism inside that makes the sound of a cricket!)

❀ Let's Talk:
Ask children to think about the sounds different animals make and the reasons why the animals might make these sounds. For example: birds sing, cats meow, bees buzz, and crickets chirp. A cricket chirps to let other crickets know where it is. Ask the children how they let other people know where *they* are. Then have them try out their sounds. You can also lead children in a discussion of when it's appropriate to be quiet (when someone is sleeping, in the library, when someone else is talking).

❀ Let's Learn:
Crickets are small insects that can be found in grasses and low shrubs. They have two large eyes and long back legs used for jumping. Crickets make a chirping sound by rubbing their two forewings together. This sound is used to attract their mates and to let them know their location. Male crickets send messages to the females. When a female hears a mating song, she moves in the direction of the "singer."

If possible, bring in a live cricket for children to listen to, feed, and observe. Crickets are often available (as snake food) at pet stores. There might be crickets in your schoolyard that children can listen for—or have the children listen in their own areas when they are at home at night. Show pictures of crickets from the books listed in the **Nonfiction Resources** at the end of the book, so that children can become familiar with this interesting insect's appearance.

CRICKETS

Let's Create: A Cricket Orchestra

❀ **What You Need:**
Cricket and instrument patterns (p. 21), heavy paper, scissors, crayons, Popsicle sticks, glue

❀ **What You Do:**
1. Duplicate the cricket and instrument patterns onto heavy paper and cut out.
2. Give each child a pattern to color and glue to a Popsicle stick.
3. Let children choose an instrument for their cricket to play. They can color this pattern and glue it to the cricket.
4. When the stick puppets have dried, ask the children to sit with them on the rug.
5. Teach children the cricket song at the end of the chapter, and let them sing it while they manipulate their puppets.

Option 1: Play a variety of music to match the instruments. If possible, bring in real examples of the instruments for children to observe. Or invite older children to come in and play. Possible recordings: "Peter and the Wolf," "A Young Person's Guide to the Orchestra," or "Carnival of the Animals."

Option 2: Discuss the different types of sounds that animals make. Then separate the children into buzzing bees, meowing cats, barking dogs, mooing cows, chirping crickets, and so on. Children can "sing" a round in their chosen voice. Or sing a round of "Old MacDonald," adding to the animals on the farm.

CRICKET MUSICIANS

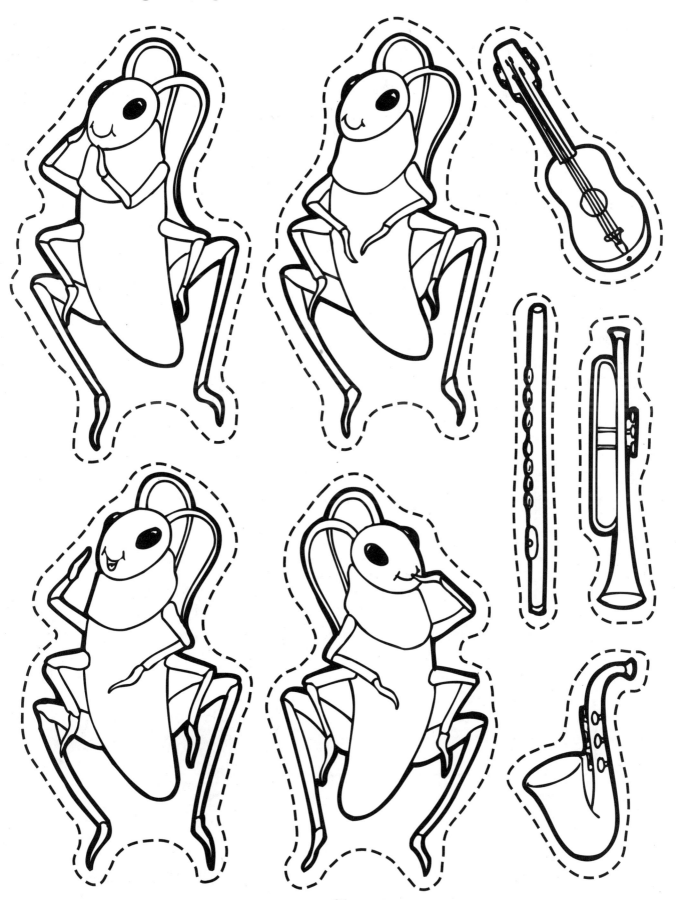

CRICKETS

Let's Create: A Camouflaged Cricket

❀ What You Need:
Cricket patterns from previous activity (without instruments); drawing paper; markers, crayons, or tempera paints (with brushes) in various shades of brown, tan, and black; glue; scissors

❀ What You Do:
1. Give each child a sheet of paper to decorate to look like a field. Provide markers, crayons, or paints in various shades of brown.
2. Give each child a few cricket patterns to glue to their picture.
3. Explain to the children that crickets are able to hide from animals or insects that might want to eat them by blending in with their environment. Children can help their crickets blend in by coloring them the same shades as the wheat, twigs, and bushes in their pictures.
4. Post finished pictures on a "Hiding Crickets" bulletin board.

Option: Cover the bulletin board ahead of time in brown and green paper. Use a similar shade of crepe paper for the border.

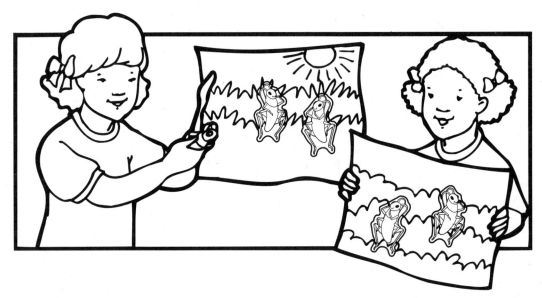

CRICKETS

Let's Find Out: How Crickets Talk

❃ **What You Need:**
Cricket patterns (below)

❃ **What You Do:**
1. Enlarge and duplicate the cricket patterns below.
2. Show the children the cricket patterns and tell them each cricket's name.
3. Teach the children the noises each kind of cricket makes.
4. Hold up the patterns separately and have the children make the right noises.
5. Separate the children into black field crickets, tree crickets, and mole crickets.
6. Remind each group which noise they make, then begin a round with each group making the correct noises.

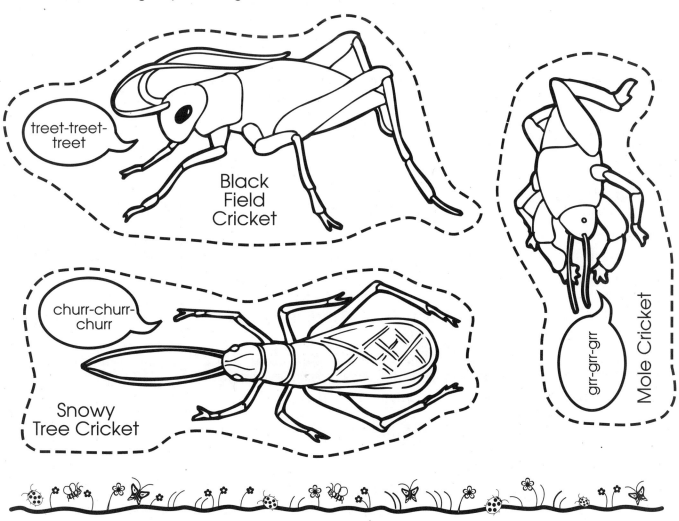

treet-treet-treet

Black Field Cricket

churr-churr-churr

Snowy Tree Cricket

grr-grr-grr

Mole Cricket

Let's Play: The Very <u>Noisy</u> Cricket Circle

In order to hear a cricket chirping, children must be very quiet.

❀ **What You Need:**
Nothing

❀ **What You Do:**
1. Have your children sit in a circle with their eyes closed.
2. Tap a child on the head and have him or her "chirp."
3. Ask the rest of the children to point toward where they hear a cricket chirping. Or have them open their eyes and guess who was making the sound.
4. Continue, moving around the circle and tapping different children.

Let's Play: Cricket Camouflage

This activity may help children further understand the meaning of "camouflage."

❀ **What You Need:**
Sheets of colored construction paper, tape

❀ **What You Do:**
1. Tape different colored sheets of construction paper to the wall at child level.
2. One at a time, have children stand in front of the sheets of paper.
3. Have the other children observe. Then have them say when the child is standing in front of paper that most closely match the clothes he or she is wearing.
4. Ask children to think of other ways people could blend in with their surroundings: painting their faces, wearing items glued to clothing that would help them blend in.

CRICKETS

Let's Sing: Cricket Songs

A Cricket Song

(to the tune of "You Are My Sunshine")

I hear a cricket,
A noisy cricket.
It keeps on chirping
All through the night.
It's past my bedtime,
But I'm not sleeping,
Because that cricket
Will chirp 'til it's light!

I'm a Little Cricket

(to the tune of "I'm a Little Teapot")

I'm a little cricket,
I sing songs.
If you know the tune,
Please sing along.
When the moon is out,
I start to play,
Rub my wings
And sing away!

LADYBUGS

Introduction

❋ **Let's Read:**

The Grouchy Ladybug by Eric Carle (Crowell, 1977).
The Grouchy Ladybug wants to pick a fight. It challenges another, friendlier ladybug and then moves on to a yellow jacket, a stag beetle, and a praying mantis. Finally, it meets its match when it gives a WHALE some lip!

❋ **Let's Talk:**

Ladybugs are believed to be lucky. One source says this is because they don't bite or sting, the way many other insects do (bees, mosquitoes, and fleas, to name a few). Ask the children to brainstorm other items that are supposed to be lucky, for example, a rabbit's foot, a four-leaf clover, or a special penny. Invite the children to bring in their own lucky charms for "Show and Tell." Or they can draw pictures of their lucky items. Post completed pictures on an "As Luck Would Have It . . ." bulletin board.

❋ **Let's Learn:**

Ladybugs are friendly insects. There are many kinds of ladybugs, and they come in different colors. The common ladybug is red and has seven black spots. The ladybug has two pairs of wings. Its hard red outer wings protect the transparent wings the ladybug uses to fly. Ladybugs eat aphids, which are very small insects that destroy plants and flowers.

Show children pictures of ladybugs in some of the nonfiction books listed at the end of this book. Then have the children observe a few of the many different types of beetles that exist in nature.

LADYBUGS

Let's Create: A Home for a Ladybug

Because your children may want to help lucky ladybugs, they can create their very own home for their very own ladybug.

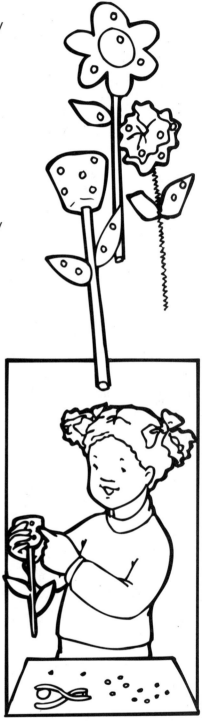

❈ **What You Need:**
Red construction paper, black crayons and markers, hole punch, individual sections of egg cartons, tempera paint, brushes, tissue paper, green pipe cleaners, glue

❈ **What You Do:**
1. Teach the children the Mother Goose rhyme (p. 34).
2. Then discuss the fact that ladybugs have new homes every day: a leaf on a rose bush, the stem of a house plant, or in the center of a daisy.
3. Provide a variety of materials for children to use to make flowers. For example, an egg carton section painted with tempera can be a lovely tulip. Crumpled tissue paper squares can become carnations or rose buds when a green pipe cleaner stem is added. Show children a few different ways to make flowers, and then let them create their own. (Help attach the pipe cleaner stems for children who have difficulty.)
4. Give each child a chance to make ladybugs by using a hole punch and red construction paper.
5. Show children how to dot their ladybugs with a black marker or crayon.
6. Children can glue as many ladybugs as they'd like to their flower homes.

Book Link:
• *Lucky Ladybugs* by Gladys Conklin, drawings by Glen Rounds (Holiday House, 1968).
This informative book focuses on the Mother Goose rhyme "Ladybug, Ladybug." And it's fun to read.

LADYBUGS

Let's Create: Ladybug Luck

Ladybugs are supposed to be good luck, and so are pennies. This craft incorporates both!

❀ What You Need:
Circle patterns (below), pennies (one for each child in the room), red and black construction paper, scissors, black markers, glue

❀ What You Do:
1. Use the patterns provided at the bottom of the page to make red and black construction paper circles, one of each for each child.
2. Give each child one circle cut from red construction paper.
3. Let the children add dots with black markers. (Common ladybugs have seven spots.)
4. Give each child a black construction paper circle and a penny.
5. Show the children how to glue the penny to the black construction paper circle, and the red construction paper circle to the top (making a penny "sandwich").
6. Once the ladybugs have dried, children can keep them in their pockets for luck!

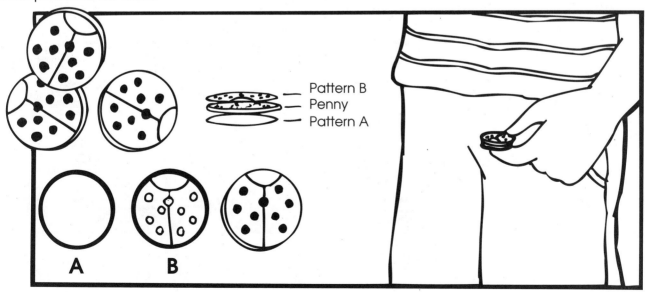

Pattern B
Penny
Pattern A

A B

LADYBUGS

Let's Find Out: About Two Sets of Wings

❀ What You Need:
Ladybug wing pattern (next page), red construction paper, clear cellophane (Contac paper may be substituted), black crayons or markers, tape, scissors

❀ What You Do:
1. Duplicate the wing pattern onto red construction paper. Make one for each child.
2. Use the pattern to cut a clear cellophane oval for each child.
3. Show the children how to tape the paper and cellophane ovals together with the red paper on top, using one piece of tape (like a hinge).
4. Give the children black crayons or markers to use to decorate the ladybug's red shell.
5. Help children cut along the line in the center toward the tape, but not through the tape. This will separate the ladybug's wings.
6. The children can see how the red shell protects the clear wings of their ladybugs.
7. Let the children give their ladybugs a good home.

Option: Provide pipe cleaners or pieces of straws for children to glue to their ladybugs as antennae.

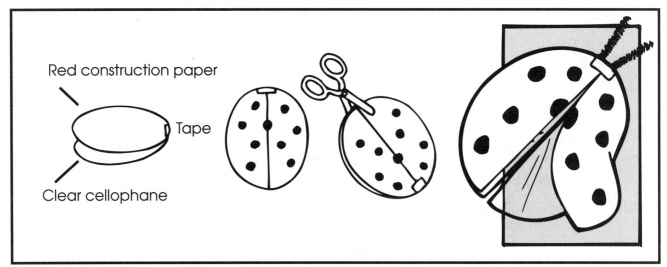

LADYBUG WINGS

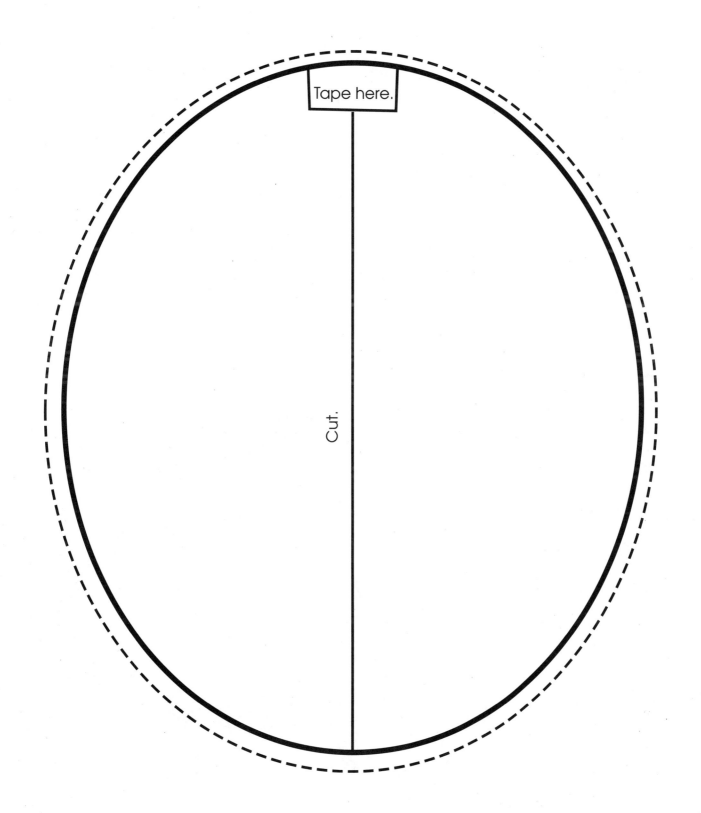

Tape here.

Cut.

LADYBUGS

Let's Play: Aphid, Aphid, Ladybug

This game is played like "Duck, Duck, Goose."

❀ What You Need:
Nothing

❀ What You Do:
1. Have the children sit in a circle.
2. Choose one child to be the ladybug.
3. This child walks around the circle, touching each of the other children on the head (gently), and saying, "Aphid, aphid, aphid . . . ladybug."
4. The tapped "ladybug" chases the first ladybug around the circle. If the tapper can sit in the vacated spot before being tagged, then the chaser is the new "ladybug." Otherwise, the tapper must go to the center of the circle, which is called the "rose bush."
5. Play continues with the new "ladybug."

LADYBUGS

Let's Sing: Ladybug Songs

Ladybug
(to the tune of "This Old Man")

Ladybug, show your spots.
You have red wings and black dots.
We will count those seven dots
On your shiny shell.
Ladybug, your spots are swell!

Ladybug, red and black,
Show those spots upon your back.
We will count those seven dots
On your shiny shell.
Ladybug, your spots are swell!

I'm a Hungry Aphid
(to the tune of "I'm a Little Teapot")

I'm a hungry aphid.
Watch me eat.
Tender little flowers
Are my treat!
When I'm in your garden
I have lunch.
I eat your roses,
Munch, munch, munch!

LADYBUGS

Let's Learn: Mother Goose Rhymes

Ladybug, Ladybug

Ladybug, ladybug,
Fly away home.
Your house is on fire.
Your children are gone.

All except one
And that's little Ann
And she has crept under
The frying pan.

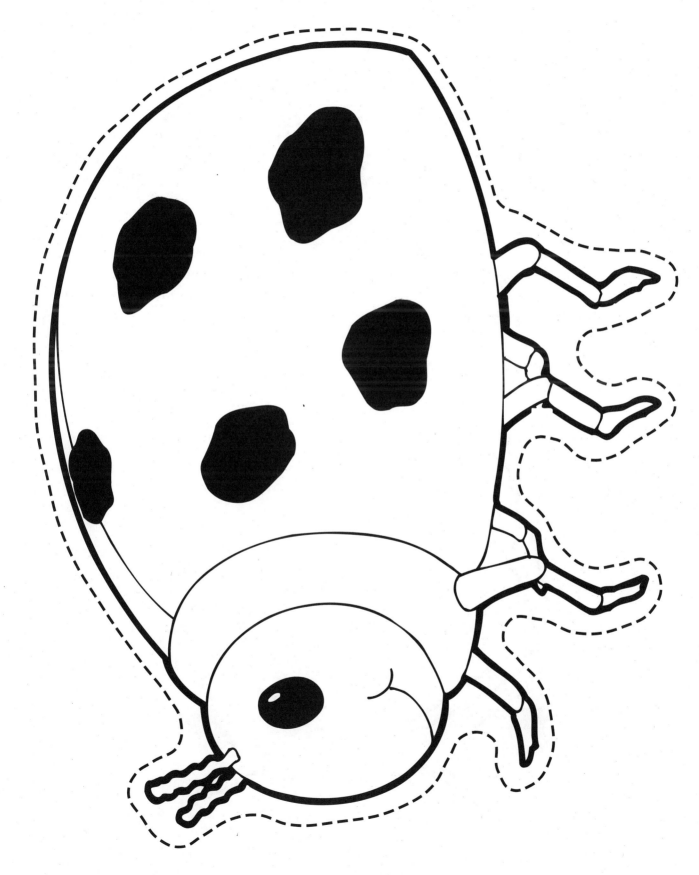

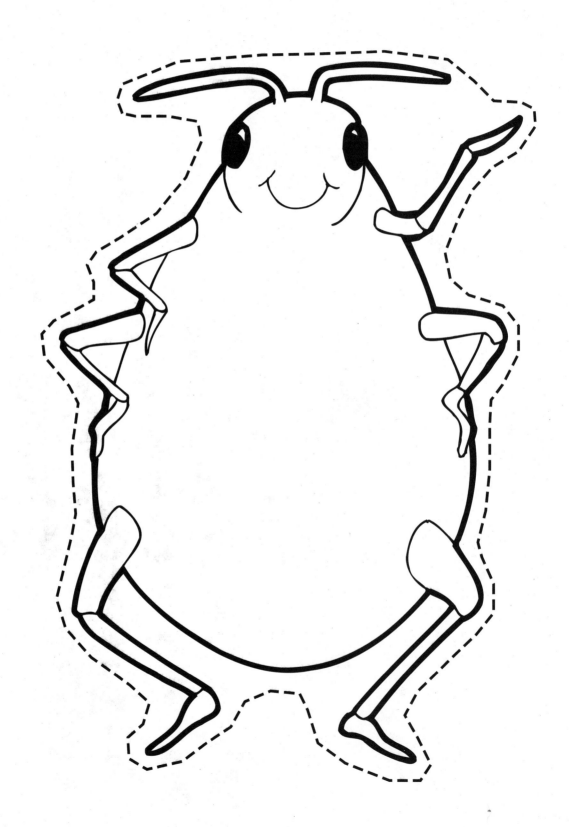

MOSQUITOES

Introduction

✽ Let's Read:
Why Mosquitoes Buzz in People's Ears: A West African Tale by Verna Aardema (Dial, 1975). A Caldecott Award winner (1976).
This book answers the age-old question: Why do mosquitoes buzz in people's ears? In this version, Mosquito, responsible for the death of Mother Owl's baby, buzzes to ask for forgiveness. This book is also available on video (Weston Woods, 1984).

✽ Let's Talk:
Discuss the story, concentrating on the fact that Mosquito feels sorry for what he did. Ask the children to brainstorm other ways to express this emotion (aside from buzzing). Children can relate a time that they did something they were sorry for. Or have them think of a situation in which someone apologized to them. The story is also about misunderstanding and blaming. Emphasize the importance of talking about problems with your children.

✽ Let's Learn:
Mosquitoes are often found near water. The female mosquitoes feed on the blood of animals and people, while the males eat plant juices. Mosquitoes really buzz with their wings, not their "mouths." A mosquito's buzz is actually a high-pitched whine, a noise made when the insect beats its wings. Mosquitoes beat their wings approximately 600 times a second!

MOSQUITOES

Let's Create: A Mosquito Mural

❀ **What You Need:**
Butcher paper, tempera paints, paintbrushes, masking tape

❀ **What You Do:**
1. Once you've read *Why Mosquitoes Buzz . . .* to the children, talk about the chain of events in the story. One animal speaks to another animal, who speaks to another, and so on. This is sort of like the game "Telephone" that children may have played.
2. Have the children make a mural of the events in the story. Help them to plan the mural, deciding who is going to work on which animal.
3. Tape the butcher paper to a hard working surface or the floor.
4. Make sure each child has a chance to work on part of the mural.
5. Once the animals have all been painted, children can add to the background, painting on trees, clouds, the sun, and so on.
6. After the mural has dried, post it in your room or in the hallway of your school. On a nearby table, display the book *Why Mosquitoes Buzz. . .*
7. List the painters' names on a sheet of paper nearby.

Option: Children can copy the style of art used in the book, adopting the same hues of paints and the angular shapes of the pictures.

MOSQUITOES

Let's Find Out: How to Avoid Mosquito Bites

Ask children if they've ever heard a mosquito buzzing. Have the children make the sound together, buzzing to each other. Ask if any of the children has ever been "bitten" by a mosquito. If so, have the children share their experiences. (Where were they—camping, on a boat, at home? What happened?)

❊ What You Need:
Mosquito netting (or a thin sheet, hammock, or volleyball net), two chairs

❊ What You Do:
1. Bring in mosquito netting for children to observe.
2. Ask the children to guess its use.
3. Drape the netting over two chairs.
4. Then let a child sit or lie under the netting.
5. The rest of the children can pretend to be mosquitoes who cannot get through the netting. They can buzz angrily around the "safe" child. (Children can take turns at this.)

Option: Discuss other methods of keeping mosquitoes at bay. Children who have been camping will know of insect-repellent sprays. You can also describe the herbal and plant-based methods of repelling mosquitoes, such as the use of eucalyptus candles.

MOSQUITOES

Let's Play: Mosquitoes Buzz

Have the children brainstorm insects that make "buzz" sounds. If they get stuck, remind them of the mosquito, bee, and fly.

❀ **What You Need:**
Why Mosquitoes Buzz in People's Ears: A West African Tale by Verna Aardema (Dial, 1975).

❀ **What You Do:**
1. Have the children sit in a circle and re-read the story aloud. Once it's very familiar to the children, it will be easier for them to participate in this game.
2. Choose one child to pretend to be the mosquito, another to pretend to be the owl, and so on for all the characters in *Why Mosquitoes Buzz....*
3. Let the children reenact the tale together, assisting them with the plot if they have trouble remembering the order of the story.
4. Let the children take turns playing the different parts.

Option: Put on a "musical" production of this story with each animal represented by a different instrument. The children choose the instruments ahead of time, then one child plays each instrument when the animal is mentioned in the story.

MOSQUITOES

Let's Sing: Mosquito Songs

Mosquitoes Like to Buzz
(to the tune of "The Farmer in the Dell")

Mosquitoes like to buzz,
Mosquitoes like to buzz,
They buzz each time they flap their wings,
And sometimes just because.

Oh, Mosquito
(to the tune of "Oh, Susannah")

Mosquitoes buzz,
They buzz and buzz,
Each time they flap their wings.
They buzz until they're close enough
To get you with their stings.

Oh, mosquito,
Oh, don't you buzz at me,
Or I'll have to go to my school
With a bandage on my knee.

Mosquitoes Are Quite Pesky Insects
(to the tune of "My Bonnie Lies Over the Ocean")

Mosquitoes are quite pesky insects.
They buzz and they buzz through the night.
And when you're asleep they come flying
To swallow a big, juicy bite (a bite!)

Don't bite, oh, don't bite, oh,
Please don't come biting at me, at me.
Don't bite, oh, don't bite, oh,
Don't take a bite out of me!

"I'M A MOSQUITO"

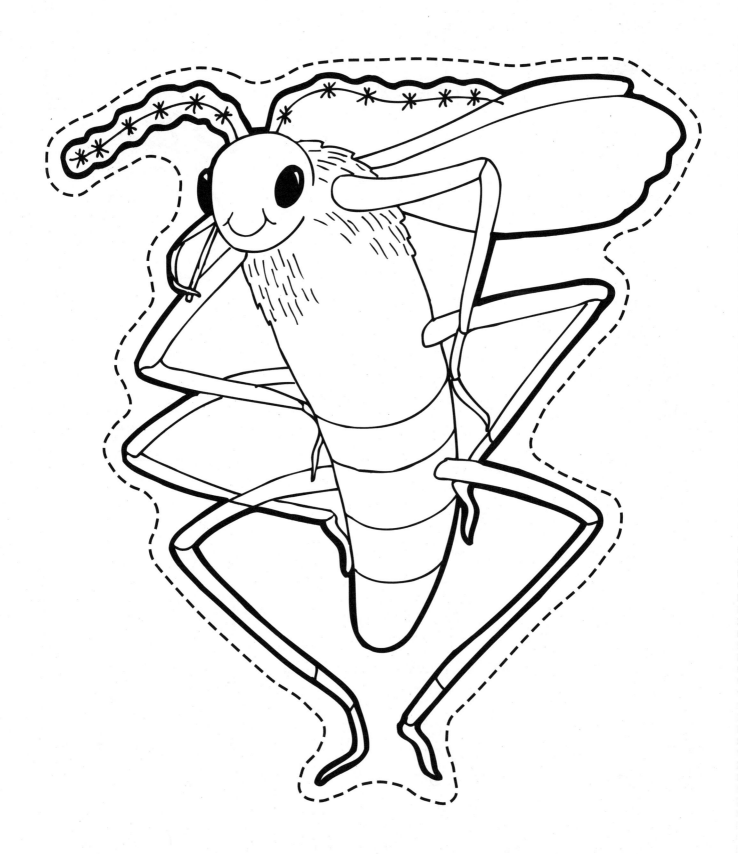

FIREFLIES

Introduction

✿ Let's Read:

A Firefly Named Torchy by Bernard Waber (Houghton Mifflin, 1970).
Torchy's light is much brighter than the other fireflies'. In fact, it's so bright that he lights up the entire forest! The other insects and animals yell at him to "Turn off that light!" Wise Old Owl tells Torchy that he's special, even if he can't twinkle the same way his peers do. (This is an important lesson for all children!)

✿ Let's Talk:

After reading the story, have children think of reasons why each of them is special. Help them brainstorm by listing different skills and having children add to the list. For example, children may think they're special because they have an older or younger sibling, or because they can tie their shoes, or count to ten, or climb to the top of the slide! Make a list of the special things your children can do!

✿ Let's Learn:

Fireflies are not really flies. They are beetles. Fireflies have an organ, called a "lantern," that makes their light. They use this light to "talk" to other fireflies. The messages they send out are actually signals to find mates.

FIREFLIES

Let's Create: A Night of Lightning Bugs

❀ **What You Need:**
Hole punches, black construction paper, tape, light-colored crayons and pencils

❀ **What You Do:**
1. Give each child a chance to punch out holes from a sheet of black construction paper using a hole punch. The children can fold the sheet in half and then punch in order to get holes in the middle of the page.
2. Explain that these holes represent the "lights" on a lightning bug. Children can use crayons to draw a bug's body around the hole punch. They can also color in a night scene, including a moon, stars, and so on. Light-colored crayons or pencils work well on the black paper.
3. Tape the pictures to a window so that the light shines through the holes. Children can observe their lightning bugs coming to life!

Note: To further enhance the effect of the light shining through the holes, make a "box" around the picture to block out the light from the sides. This can be done by folding up the edges of the picture.

Option: Provide sheets of aluminum foil or silver paper for children to glue or tape to the backs of their pictures. The foil will make the lightning bugs' "lights" shine.

FIREFLIES

Let's Create: Fingerprint Fireflies

Children who've never seen fireflies can picture different kinds of bursts of light they might have seen in the night sky: falling stars, beacon lights, or fireworks, perhaps.

✿ What You Need:
Finger paints (including white and yellow), colored paper (black or dark blue works well), glue, glitter, markers

✿ What You Do:
1. Give each child a sheet of paper.
2. Tell children that they can use their imaginations to create firefly displays on their papers. They can make a firefly shape by just spotting the paper with the tips of their paint-dipped fingers.
3. Provide glitter and glue for children to use to decorate the completed pictures. The glitter can make the fireflies twinkle!
4. Post the completed pictures on a "Fantastic Firefly" bulletin board.

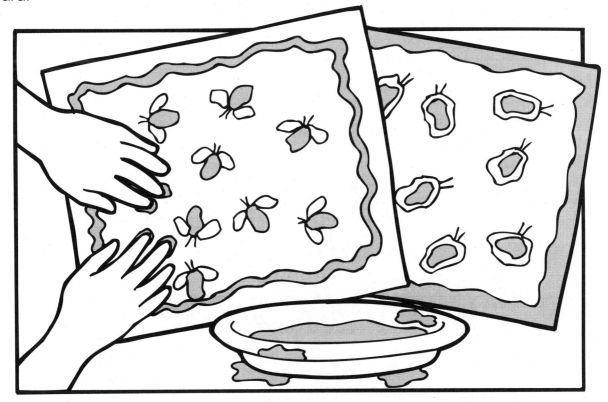

FIREFLIES

Let's Find Out: What Lightning Bugs Look Like

Fireflies don't exist in all parts of the country. If your children have never seen a firefly, this activity will help them understand the magic of these insects!

❀ **What You Need:**
Small white Christmas tree lights (the type that blink on and off)

❀ **What You Do:**
1. String the lights around the room.
2. Have the children sit in a circle in the middle of the room.
3. Describe what lightning bugs look like. If possible show pictures from a nonfiction book (see the **Nonfiction Resources** section at the end of the book). Or read a picture book, such as *Fireflies!* by Julie Brinckloe (Macmillan, 1985).
4. Dim (or turn off) the lights.
5. Describe a typical scene in which the children might find lightning bugs. For example, have them imagine that they are in a meadow at twilight. The sun has just set and the lightning bugs are beginning to wink on and off in the darkness.
6. Turn on the blinking lights and let children observe them.

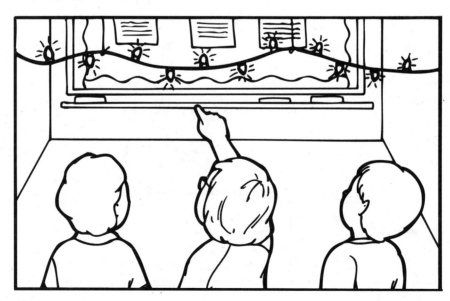

FIREFLIES

Let's Find Out: How Fireflies "Talk"

❀ **What You Need:**
Two flashlights

❀ **What You Do:**
1. Explain to your children that fireflies signal to each other in special ways. A male flashes three, four, or five quick flashes. A female answers with one, two, or three.
2. Bring two flashlights into the room and give one to one of your children. (Keep the other.)
3. Dim the lights in the room.
4. Have the child send "lightning bug" flashes with his or her light.
5. Answer the beam with your own flashlight.
6. Now, move around the room and try the experiment again.
7. Afterwards, ask the children if they knew where the two flashing "bugs" were and, if so, how they could tell.
8. Let other children have a chance flashing the lights.

Note: If the room is too light, drape a blanket over some chairs to create a dark space. A few children at a time can try this activity in the space.

FIREFLIES

Let's Play: Thousands of Fireflies

❀ What You Need:
Small mirrors, flashlight

❀ What You Do:
1. Show children how to angle the mirrors to reflect a glare of sun around the room.
2. Let children take turns focusing the light from the mirrors and making it dance across the walls.

Let's Play: Find the Firefly

❀ What You Need:
Nothing

❀ What You Do:
1. Have the children play this game like "Sardines." One child hides and the rest try to find the missing "firefly."
2. When each child finds the "firefly," he or she joins the firefly in the hiding place.
3. The last child to find the group becomes the first to hide in the next round.

FIREFLIES

Let's Sing: Lightning Bug
(to the tune of "You Are My Sunshine")

I'm like a "lite brite,"
I have a night light.
I fly in circles, up in the sky.
Some call me "lightning,"
When my light's blinking.
But to my friends, I'm just "firefly."

While others sleep tight,
I flash my night light,
I fill the dark sky with light so bright.
Look out your window,
You'll see me flashing,
And then I'll turn off and tell you
      "good night."

"I'M A FIREFLY"

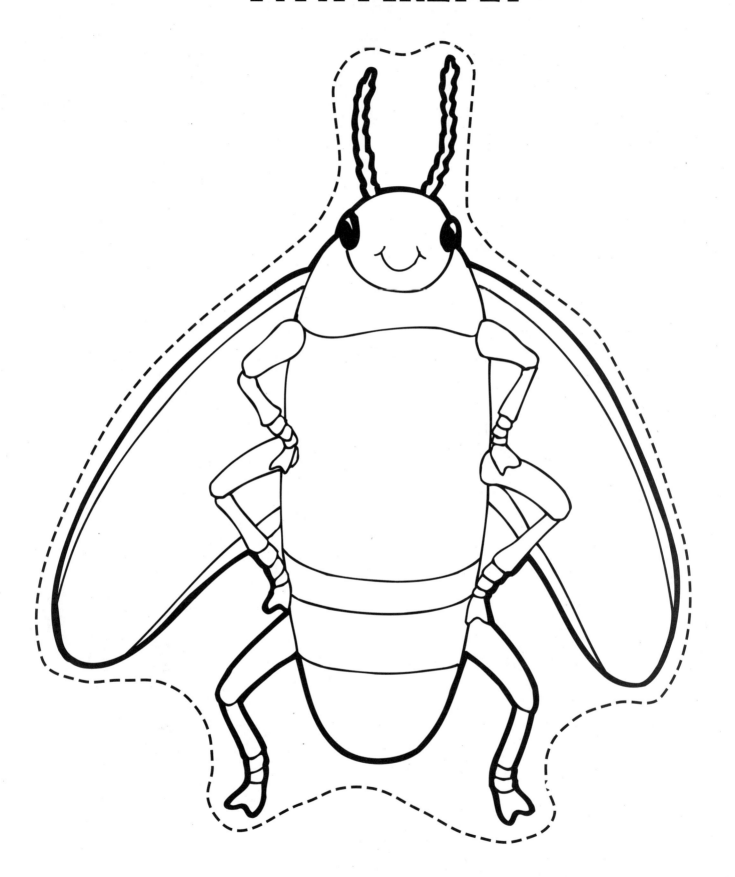

GRASSHOPPERS

Introduction

❁ **Let's Read:**
Grasshopper on the Road by Arnold Lobel (Harper and Row, 1978).
Grasshopper wanted to go on a journey. "I will find a road," he said. "I will follow that road wherever it goes." Grasshopper's journey takes him by a group of beetles who only like the morning, a housefly with a cleaning fixation, a bevy of butterflies who never alter their routine, a silly mosquito, some quick-flying dragonflies, and others.

❁ **Let's Talk:**
Ask your children if they've ever taken a journey. Invite them to share their experiences. Then describe a trip you've taken. As a group, take a small trip outside (to the playground or around the block). Children can hunt for "little living things" and other insects along the way. When you come back to the room, discuss the various things you saw on your journey and write a story about your trip "on the road."

❁ **Let's Learn:**
A grasshopper is an insect that feeds on grass. Grasshoppers are good at jumping and flying. They have many enemies, including frogs, toads, birds, and cats. Luckily, grasshoppers blend into their surroundings because they are the same color as grass.

GRASSHOPPERS

Let's Create: Can You Find the Grasshopper?

❋ **What You Need:**
Grasshopper patterns (p. 53), green crayons, green watercolors, paintbrushes, plain paper, glue, scissors

❋ **What You Do:**
1. Have children cut out the grasshopper patterns and glue them to the plain paper.
2. Provide crayons for children to use to color the grasshoppers.
3. Set out watercolors and brushes for children to use to make watercolor "resist" pictures: painting over the already colored grasshoppers.
4. Let the pictures dry, then post on a bulletin board labeled "Can You Find the Grasshoppers?"

Version 2:
Grasshopper patterns, paper or thin cardboard, blades of grass, leaves, twigs, glue, old magazines, paper, crayons or markers, scissors

1. Duplicate the grasshopper patterns and cut out.
2. Give each child a sheet of paper or thin cardboard to use to create a meadow scene. The children can glue grass, leaves, and twigs to the paper, or they can cut out these images from magazines.
3. Let the children position the grasshoppers under the leaves, on the undersides of the blades of grass, and along the twigs.
4. Children can use crayons or markers in various shades of green to color the grasshoppers to match the surroundings.
5. Post completed pictures on a bulletin board.

Option: Cover the bulletin board with green wrapping paper ahead of time. Bring in dried grasses to use for a border.

~ GRASSHOPPER PATTERNS ~

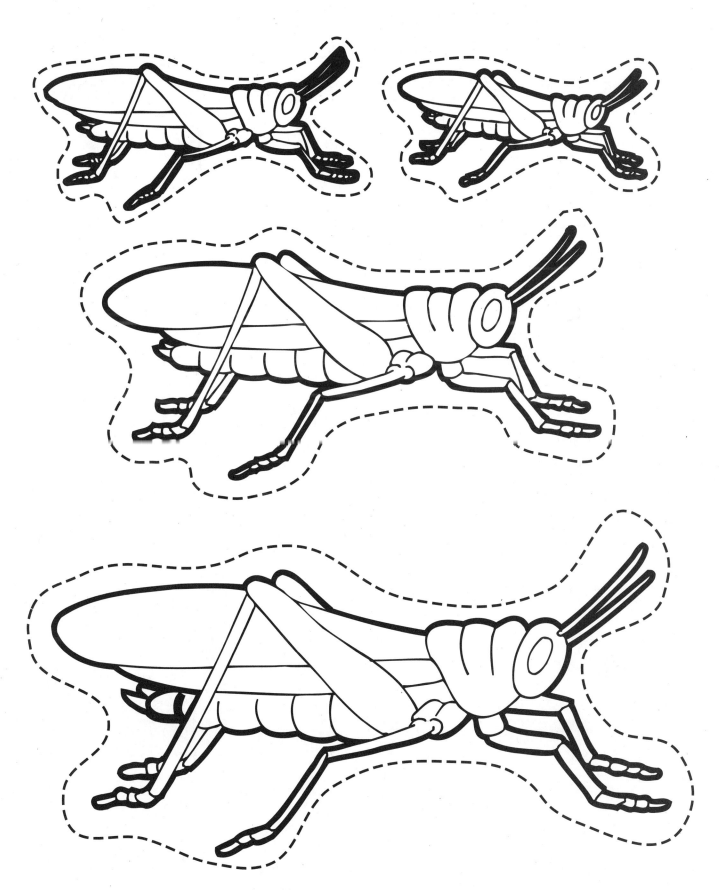

GRASSHOPPERS

Let's Find Out: Who Likes the Day?

Grasshoppers and crickets are like cousins. They look very similar and share many characteristics. One difference, however, is the fact that grasshoppers like the day while crickets come out at night. In *Grasshopper on the Road*, Grasshopper meets other insects who think the day is best!

✽ **What You Need:**
Grasshopper postcard patterns (p. 55), crayons or markers

✽ **What You Do:**
1. Discuss journeys with the children. Explain that grasshoppers like to be out in the day, while crickets are out at night.
2. Duplicate the postcard patterns and give one to each child to color with the appropriate scene: day for grasshopper, night for cricket.
3. Children can dictate messages for the backs of the cards. Or they can write notes to friends or draw pictures.
4. Distribute the cards to the addressees, or post them on a "Night & Day" bulletin board.

Option: Use sun and moon cutouts to decorate the border of your bulletin board. (Enlarge from the patterns on p. 55.)

GRASSHOPPERS

Let's Play: Hop-a-LONG Grasshopper

Discuss how good grasshoppers are at jumping. Then have the children pretend to be "Happy Hoppers!"

✿ **What You Need:**
Yardstick, chalk

✿ **What You Do:**
1. Have children take turns jumping as far as they can.
2. Mark their jumps with a piece of chalk.
3. Measure the jumps with the yardstick.
4. Encourage children to go for a "personal best" and not to compete with each other.

Variation: Challenge the children to find out how many jumps it takes to get across the room. Or, if you're outside, they can see how many jumps it takes them to get from the fence to the slide, and so on.

GRASSHOPPERS

Let's Sing: Grasshopper Songs

The Grasshopper Song
(to the tune of "Jingle Bells")

Grasshopper, grasshopper, grasshopper
    so green.
You're the greatest hopper, I have ever seen.
Grasshopper, grasshopper, grasshopper
    so green.
You're the greatest hopper, I have ever seen.

The Grasshopper, He Hops Along
(to the tune of "The Ants Go Marching One by One")

The grasshopper, he hops along,
He hops—he hops.
The grasshopper, he hops and never stops,
    he hops.
The grasshopper, he hops along,
Never stopping to hear my song,
He just keeps on hopping on,
And he hops,
Yes, he hops.
(Hop, hop, hop.)

"I'M A GRASSHOPPER"

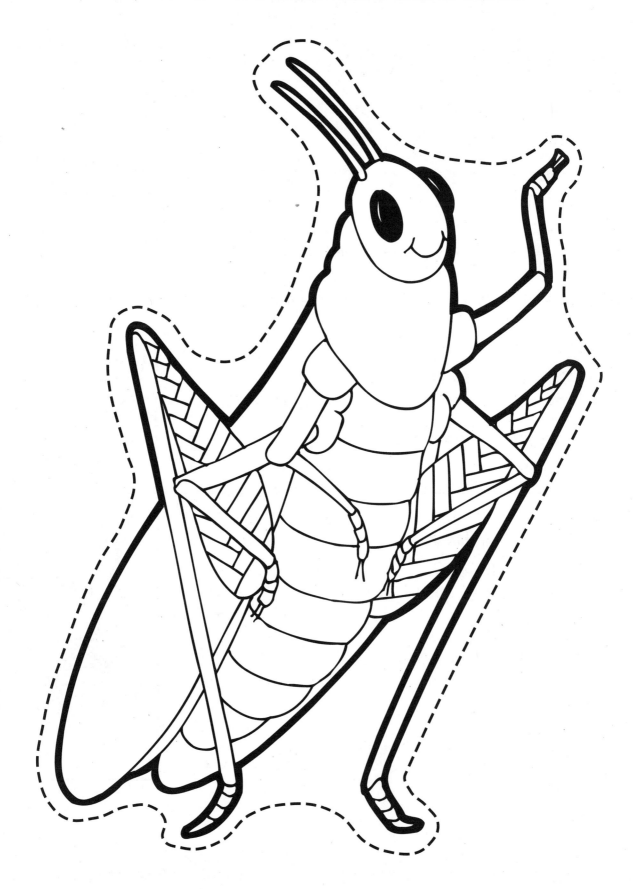

BEES

Introduction

❀ Let's Read:

Fiona's Bee by Beverly Keller, pictures by Diane Patterson
(Coward, 1975).
A lonely girl rescues a bee from drowning and suddenly finds
herself with lots of new friends. This book is also available as a
sound recording (Listening Library, 1981).

❀ Let's Talk:

Children who are shy may really open up to this story. Have
children discuss a time when they felt shy and how they
were able to get over this feeling. Stage a "Show and Tell" in
which children bring in items that are important to them
("transitional objects"—blankets or teddy bears). Talking
about something they like and know about can help children
get over any shyness. (This would also be an appropriate time
to discuss being a new person in a school or neighborhood.)

❀ Let's Learn:

After visiting up to 100 different flowers, honeybees go back
to the hive and spit up the nectar they have swallowed.
Worker bees mix this substance with their saliva and then
store it in combs, where it eventually thickens into what is
known as honey. The bees eat this store of food in winter and
also use it to feed their young.

BEES

Let's Create: Bumblebees

Bees have three body parts: a head, a thorax, and an abdomen. They also have six legs, four wings, and hairy bodies. There are two feelers, or antennae, on the front of a bee's head. The bee uses them to touch things (and for smelling, too, since it has no nose)!

✿ What You Need:

Yarn or markers (black and yellow), empty spools or corks or film canisters (photo stores will often donate these), black pipe cleaners, scissors, quarter-sized circles cut from clear Contac paper, glue, scissors

✿ What You Do:

1. Show children how to make bumblebees by covering a spool or cork with glue and then wrapping sections with yellow and black yarn to make stripes. (Children can also color spools or corks with black and yellow markers.)
2. Cut short sections of black pipe cleaners for children to glue to their bees for antennae.
3. Four small circles of Contac paper will stick right on for the bees' wings. (Bees have two sets of wings.)
4. Save some bees for use with beehives (p. 61).

Let's Create: Beehives

❀ **What You Need:**
Yarn (tan or brown), glue, empty juice cans, cork bees (see previous activity)

❀ **What You Do:**
1. Show children how to coat an empty, washed juice can with glue and then wrap the can with tan-colored yarn to make a hive.
2. When the hives have dried, children can glue their bees to the outside of the hives.
3. Set the completed bees and hives on a table covered with brown paper. For display, place a stick or branch with leaves nearby, positioned so that the hives look as if they are attached to it. Set up Winnie the Pooh books nearby.

Option 1: Let the children color the hive pattern (p. 62) with crayons and markers and glue their bees to it.

Option 2: Children can decorate empty egg cartons as honeycombs and the bees can be displayed there.

Book Link: *Look At Homes, Holes and Hives* by Henry Pluckrose (Franklin Watts, 1990).
There are many types of houses for humans, and many types for insects as well. This book pictures wild honeybee nests and domestic beehives.

BEEHIVE PATTERN

BEES

Let's Find Out: How Bees Give Directions

Bees dance to tell other bees which way to go to the flowers and how far to fly. The first part of the wagging dance shows which direction to go. The second shows how far the flowers are from the hive. Bees also dance when they find a new home.

❀ What You Need:
Construction paper, scissors, pillow or beanbag chair

❀ What You Do:
1. Give children their choice of colored construction paper from which to cut out flowers.
2. Have the children position the flowers around the room.
3. Set the pillow or beanbag chair in one corner of the room. Explain that this is the "hive."
4. Have the children pretend to be bees. They start at their hive and go out in search of flowers. When they find a flower, they must tell the other bees where the flower is. They must do a "bee dance" to tell the direction to the other bees.
5. Children can experiment with their dance steps, wiggling and flapping their "wings" in order to point out the location of the flowers to each other.

Option: Play music while children perform their bee dances, such as, "Flight of the Bumblebee" by Nicolai Rimsky-Korsakov.

BEES

Let's Play: Busy Bee Concentration

❀ **What You Need:**
Concentration patterns (p. 65), markers or crayons, scissors, Contac paper (optional)

❀ **What You Do:**
1. Duplicate the cards twice, color, and cut out. Laminate or cover with Contac paper, if desired.
2. Demonstrate how to play "Concentration." The children can be "busy bees" as they turn all the cards face down. Each child turns two over at a time. If the cards match, the child keeps them. If the cards do not match, the child turns them back over and another child takes a turn.

~ CONCENTRATION PATTERNS ~

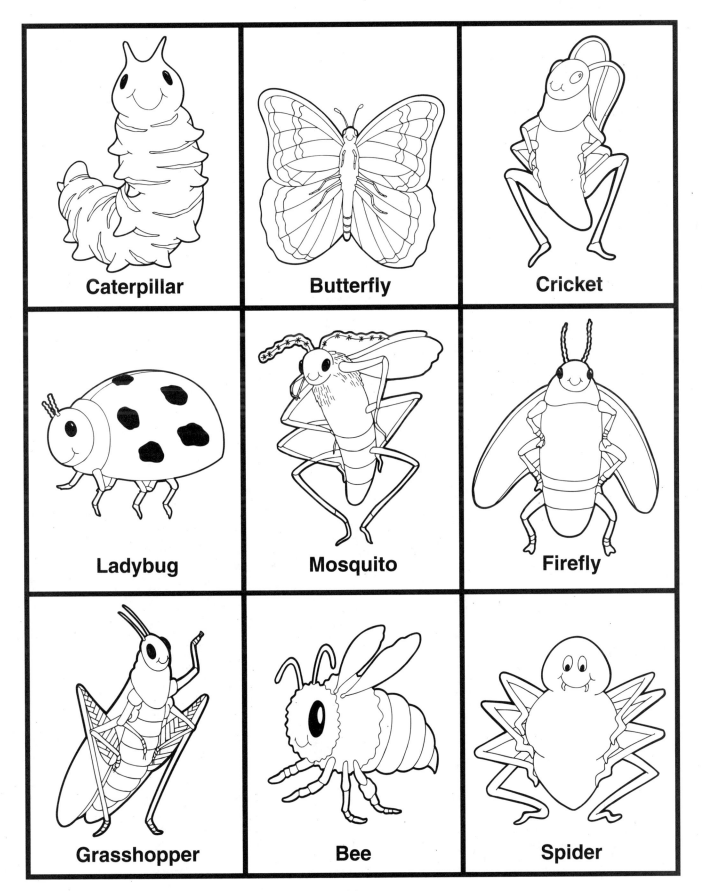

Caterpillar	Butterfly	Cricket
Ladybug	Mosquito	Firefly
Grasshopper	Bee	Spider

Let's Sing: Do You Like to Buzz?
(to the tune of "Do Your Ears Hang Low?")

Do you like to buzz,
Are you covered all in fuzz?
Do you call a hive a home
In the garden where you roam?
Do you know how to make honey,
Are your stripes a little funny?
Do you like to buzz?

BEES

Let's Learn: Mother Goose Rhymes

A Swarm of Bees in May

A swarm of bees in May
Is worth a load of hay;
A swarm of bees in June
Is worth a silver spoon;
A swarm of bees in July
Is not worth a fly.

Burnie Bee, Burnie Bee

Burnie bee, burnie bee,
Tell me when your wedding be?
If it be tomorrow day,
Take your wings and fly away.

There Was a Bee

There was a bee
Sat on a wall;
He said he could hum,
And that was all.

SPIDERS

Introduction

❀ **Let's Read:** *Miss Spider's Tea Party* by David Kirk (Scholastic, 1994).

When Miss Spider tries to host a tea party, the other bugs refuse to come for fear of being eaten. Eventually, Miss Spider is able to convince her buggy friends of her good intentions. She hosts a successful tea party, and the other insects learn that Miss Spider is a vegetarian!

❀ **Let's Talk:**

Set up a tea party in the room, and let the children take turns playing host. Each child can pretend to be one of the insects in the story. While the children drink their tea, have them discuss a time when they met new friends—perhaps the first day they went to school or day care, or at another friend's house. Talk about the importance of having friends.

❀ **Let's Learn:**

A spider is an "arachnid" and not an insect. Spiders have eight legs, two body parts, and eight eyes, while insects have three body parts and only six legs. Spiders were on earth 300 million years ago, long before the first people. There are 35,000 different kinds of spiders. Although spiders hunt other creatures for their food, very few hurt people. Some spiders in the forests of South America, Asia, and Africa are big enough to eat birds and small mammals. They have apple-size bodies and pencil-like legs.

SPIDERS

Let's Create: A HUGE Spider Web

This is a project the children can work on together.

❀ What You Need:

Insect patterns from previous chapters, dark-colored poster board, yarn, tape

❀ What You Do:

1. Tape one end of a roll of yarn to the poster board. Have the children sit around the poster board. (You can do this in small groups, a few children at a time.)
2. Hand the yarn ball to a child and let the child roll it to the other side of the poster board. Place a piece of tape on the yarn there, to fasten it.
3. Give the yarn ball to another child and let the child roll it to another side of the poster board. Place a piece of tape on the yarn there, to fasten it.
4. Continue, letting different children roll and anchor the tape to create a huge spider web on the poster board.
5. When every child has had a turn, and when the web looks finished, let each child use tape to attach one insect pattern to the spider web.
6. Tape a spider pattern (from this chapter) onto the middle of the web.
7. Post the finished project in the room.

SPIDERS

Let's Create: A Small Spider's Home

❀ **What You Need:**
Black construction paper, white or silver paint in squeeze bottles, spider lunch patterns (p. 72), "I'm a Spider" pattern (p. 76), scissors, crayons or markers, glue, clear Contac paper (optional)

❀ **What You Do:**
1. Give each child a sheet of black construction paper.
2. Children can take turns using the squeeze bottles of paint to make spider webs on their papers.
3. Duplicate the spider lunch patterns and cut out.
4. Let children choose a few patterns from the lunch patterns to color and glue to their spider's web.
5. Duplicate the "I'm a Spider" pattern, cut out, and give one to each child.
6. Children can glue their spider to a corner of the web. Help children write their names on the spider.
7. Laminate the completed pictures or cover in Contac paper. Children can take their pictures home to use for their own lunch place mats.

Variation: Do string painting. Have the children dip a short length of string or yarn into white paint, then drag the string around on the paper to make web designs. Glue can also be substituted for the paint, then sprinkled with glitter for a web fresh with "morning dew."

~ SPIDER LUNCH PATTERNS ~

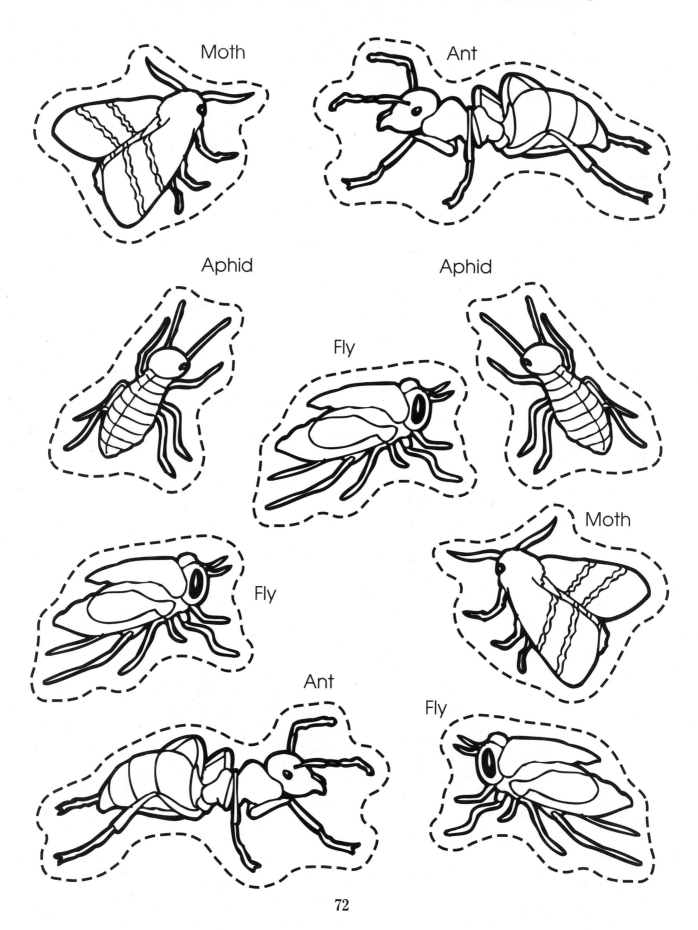

Moth

Ant

Aphid

Aphid

Fly

Fly

Moth

Ant

Fly

SPIDERS

Let's Find Out: How It Feels to Have Eight Legs

❊ **What You Need:**
Nothing

❊ **What You Do:**
1. Divide children into four-person teams.
2. Have the teams stand in lines, with each child holding onto the waist of the child in front.
3. Let the lead child in each team set the pace, walking around the room, skipping, hopping, etc. (This is like a smaller version of "Follow the Leader," except that the players are attached.)
4. Have the children rotate, each taking a turn being the leader.
5. Afterward, have the children discuss whether it was difficult or easy to move around with so many "limbs."

SPIDERS

Let's Sing: I'm a Spider
(to the tune of "Alouette")

I'm a spider,
Yes, I am a spider,
I'm a spider,
You can count my legs.
I have legs from one to eight.
I think that my legs are great.
One to eight.
(One to eight.)
I'm so great.
(I'm so great.)
Ohhh,
I'm a spider,
Yes, I am a spider,
I'm a spider,
You can count my legs.

SPIDERS

Let's Learn: Mother Goose Rhymes

Little Miss Muffet

Little Miss Muffet
Sat on a tuffet
Eating her curds and whey.
Along came a spider
Who sat down beside her
And frightened Miss Muffet away.

The Eensy Weensy Spider

The eensy weensy spider
Crawled up the waterspout.
Down came the rain and washed the spider
    out.
Out came the sun and dried up all the rain,
And the eensy weensy spider
Crawled up the spout again.

∼ STORYBOOK RESOURCES ∼

Caterpillar & Butterfly Books:
- *I Can Squash Elephants! A Masai Tale About Monsters* by Malcolm Carrick (Viking, 1978).
- *The Butterfly* by A. Delaney (Crown, 1977).
- *One Dragon to Another* by Ned Delaney (Houghton, 1976).

Cricket Books:
- *Quick As a Cricket* by Audrey Wood, illustrated by Don Wood (Child's Play,1982).
- *A Pocketful of Cricket* by Rebecca Caudill (Holt, 1964).
- *Nicholas Cricket* by Joyce Maxner (HarperCollins, 1989).
- *If I Were a Cricket...* by Kazue Mizumura (Crowell, 1973).

Ladybug Books:
- *Ladybug, Ladybug* by Ruth Brown (Dutton, 1988).
- *Ladybug, Ladybug!* by Robert Kraus (Harper, 1957).
- *Fast Is Not a Ladybug* by Miriam Schlein (Addison-Wesley, 1953).

Firefly Books:
- *The Fireflies* by Max Bolliger (Atheneum, 1970).
- *Dashiel and the Night* by Larry Callen (Dutton, 1981).
- *Sam and the Firefly* by P.D. Eastman (Random House, 1975).
- *Fireflies* by Joanne Ryder (Harper, 1977).

Grasshopper Books:
- *John J. Plenty and Fiddler Dan: A New Fable of the Grasshopper and the Ant* by John Ciardi (Lippincott, 1963).
- *Bear Circus* by William Pène Du Bois (Viking, 1971).
- *Why Worry?* by Eric A. Kimmel (Pantheon, 1979).
- *Rilloby-rill* by Sir Henry John Newbolt (O'Hara, 1973).

Bee Books:
- *Buzz, Buzz, Buzz* by Byron Barton (Macmillan, 1973).
- *The Rose in My Garden* by Arnold Lobel (Greenwillow, 1984).
- *Follow Me Cried Bee* by Jan Wahl (Crown, 1976).
- *Harry's Bee* by Peter Campbell (The Bobbs-Merrill Co., 1969).

Spider Books:
- *Spider Magic* by Chris Cahill (Schneider Educational, 1990).
- *How Spider Saved Valentine's Day* by Robert Kraus (Scholastic, 1986).
- *Anansi the Spider: A Tale from the Ashanti* by Gerald McDermott (Holt, 1972). This story is also available on video.
- *The Eency Weency Spider* by Joanne Oppenheim (Bantam, 1991).

~ NONFICTION RESOURCES ~

Caterpillar & Butterfly Books:
- *Monarch Butterfly* by Gail Gibbons (Holiday House, 1989). This book explains in simple text the stages of life of a monarch butterfly.
- *Butterfly and Caterpillar* by Barrie Watts (Silver Burdett, 1985). Color photographs and line drawings explain the life cycles of a butterfly.
- *When Insects Are Babies* by Gladys Conklin (Holiday House, 1969). Discusses tiny new baby insects and how they grow into adults.

Cricket Books:

- *Grasshoppers and Their Kin* by Ross E. Hutchins (Dodd, 1972).
- *Grasshoppers and Crickets* (Franklin Watts, 1991).
- *Chirping Insects* by Sylvia A. Johnson (Lerner, 1986).

Ladybug Books:
- *Aphids* adapted by Georgianne Heymann (Raintree Publishers, 1987).
- *The Ladybug and Other Insects: A First Discovery Book* (Scholastic, 1989). Information about ladybugs and other beetles.
- *Ladybug* by Barrie Watts (Silver Burdett, 1987). Color photos show the transformation from egg to larva to pupa to adult beetle.

Mosquito Books:
- *Mosquitoes* by Charles L. Ripper (William Morrow, 1969). Informative book for teachers to use.
- *Let's Find Out About Mosquitoes* by David Webster (Franklin Watts, 1974). Another informative resource.

Firefly Books:
- *Flash, the Life of a Firefly* by Louise Dyer Harris (Little, Brown, 1966).
- *Fireflies* by Sylvia A. Johnson (Lerner, 1986).

Grasshopper Books:
- *The Life Cycle of a Grasshopper* by Jill Bailey, illustrated by Carolyn Scrace (The Bookwright Press, 1990). Useful for teachers. Interesting pictures for children.
- *Grasshoppers* by Robert E. Pfadt, illustrated by William R. Eastman, Jr., and Jeanne Heitkamp (Follett, 1966). Life cycle and other drawings could be shown to a small group.
- *Red Legs* by Alice E. Goudey, illustrated by Marie Nonnast (Charles Scribner's Sons, 1966). Read excerpts of this factual story to the children.

Bee Books:
- *The Busy Honeybee* by Bernice Kohn (Four Winds Press, 1972).

Spider Books:
- *Spiders* by Kate Petty, illustrated by Alan Baker (Franklin Watts, 1985).
- *The Spider* by Margaret Lane, pictures by Barbara Firth (Dial, 1982).
- *The Spiders Dance* by Joanne Ryder (Harper & Row, 1981).

~ ADDITIONAL RESOURCES ~

Bugs on the "Net"
Iowa State University's Tasty Insect Recipes
(at http://www.public.iastate.edu/):
from DIRECTORY of personal and locker home pages, go to ENTOMOLOGY,
then INSECTS AS FOOD. Here you'll find recipes for "Bug Blox," "Banana Army
Worm Bread," "Rootworm Beetle Dip," and "Chocolate Chirpie Chip Cookies."

The Food Insects Newsletter
This newsletter, edited by Dr. Gene DeFoliart, is available by writing to Professor
DeFoliart c/o the Department of Entomology, 545 Russell Laboratories,
University of Wisconsin, Madison, WI 53706. It is published three times each
year. A donation of at least $5.00 is requested to help with printing costs.
Note: Tell children that insects are sometimes eaten as food in some parts of
the world.

The following recipe by Douglas Whitman and S. Sakaluk of Illinois State
University appeared in the newsletter:

Crispy Cajun Crickets
1 cup crickets (check with your local pet supply store)
1 tsp. oatmeal
paprika
salt
garlic
chili or Tabasco sauce
1 stick of butter or margarine, melted

1. Place 1 cup of healthy crickets in a large, clean, and airy container.
2. Add a pinch of oatmeal for food.
3. After one day, remove damaged crickets and freeze the remainder.
4. Wash frozen crickets in tap water, spread on cookie sheet, and roast in oven
at lowest setting.
5. When crickets are crunchy, sprinkle with butter sauce made from remaining
ingredients (add spices to taste) and serve.

Insect Cookbooks
Entertaining With Insects (Salutek Publishing, 1976).
To order the book, call 1-800-395-1351.

Fun Insect-shaped Food
Farley's "Creepy Crawlers" Fruit Snacks

~ MORE MONDAY MORNING ~ RESOURCES

The "Happy World" series encourages students to explore and respect the world around them. Students will make unique crafts, read (or listen to) interesting literature links, sing songs to familiar tunes, and play great games!

Animal Friends
Gr. PreK-1, 80 pp., MM 2012
Promote concern for endangered animals through creative early learning activities. Each animal "unit" includes a pattern of the animal that can be made into a puppet, plus a face mask of the animal.

Friends from Around the World
Gr. PreK-1, 80 pp., MM 2013
Activities such as "Glitter Letters," "Feeling Concentration," "Your Passport, Please," and "Traveling 'Round and 'Round" will encourage children to become friends with people from around the world! Patterns to duplicate and enlarge will enhance room decor.

Art from Throwaways
Gr. PreK-1, 80 pp., MM 2014
From trash to treasure, your students will tap into their creative sides while using recyclable materials! Children will love turning milk cartons into "Yellow Submarines" and paper bags into "Wild West Vests"! Included for each project are reproducible wordless directions for students.